TABLE OF CONTENTS

BEFORE
WE START

It seems rather funny to have a preface for a book on the topic of starting.

But I did want to set the stage for what you are about to read.

You see, before this became a booklet it was a sermon. On January 10th of 2022, I spoke to my church on this topic. And many who heard me speak were engaged in starting things.

Starting a marriage.
Starting a job.
Starting a new semester abroad.
Starting relationships.
Or restarting something.

And while some might say, "better than starting things right, is ending things right" I would suggest to you that both are equally important. This booklet is a primer. It is to provide you with four elements to help you lay the foundation for starting well.

You see we all start something.
Before you began to read this, your day started. Perhaps it began with a pesky shrill sound of an alarm.

Then, hopefully, it was followed by your coffee maker making that lovely dripping sound of a black elixir dropping into a carafe.

Then you started a shower. You started off to work. Or to school. Or to the grocery store. But each one of us started something.

And so, whether you are a high school student starting to think about college,
A soccer mom thinking of launching an online business or
A single person starting a brand new relationship

I hope that these pages provide you with the right framework, the right foundations for a life well lived. I would encourage you to use it for your own personal growth but we also have included some questions to process in a small group setting or with some of your close friends or family.

OK.

We're ready to start!

INTRODUCTION

"Flawed From Day One."

So read the report six forensic engineers produced to explain what happened at Miami's Chamberlain Towers when they crumbled in 2021. The engineers identified multiple structural problems that went all the way back to the original construction. Mainly, the building's pillars and columns did not meet the proper code; they were too thin, too small to accommodate the amount of rebar needed to sustain the building.

The builders sought to cut costs. As a result, 40 years later the tower went down—and took the lives of 98 people.

You've probably heard this before: "Better than starting well is ending well."

I heard that often from my mentors growing up. Now I've realized that, as necessary as it is to end well, it is vital to begin well. Each are important, of course, but it is necessary to lay the proper foundations before beginning anything. If you are getting married, ensure that you have the right foundations. If you are starting a business, make sure you have the right foundations. Before becoming a parent, make sure the right family foundations are in place to the extent that you can.

Where can we find the wisdom to build secure foundations for life?

Consider the counsel we find in Scripture. Let's read these words from the **Gospel of Mark:**

In those days Jesus came from Nazareth of Galilee and was baptized by John in the Jordan. And when he came up out of the water, immediately he saw the heavens being torn open and the Spirit descending on him like a dove. And a voice came from heaven, "You are my beloved Son; with you I am well pleased." The Spirit immediately drove him out into the wilderness. And he was in the wilderness forty days, being tempted by Satan. And he was with the wild animals, and the angels were ministering to him.

Now after John was arrested, Jesus came into Galilee, proclaiming the gospel of God, and saying, "The time is fulfilled, and the kingdom of God is at hand; repent and believe in the gospel."

Passing alongside the Sea of Galilee, he saw Simon and Andrew the brother of Simon casting a net into the sea, for they were fishermen. And Jesus said to them, "Follow me, and I will make you become fishers of men." And immediately they left their nets and followed him. **(Mark 1:9-18)**

Mark's account takes us to the beginning of Jesus' vocation, showing us the foundation of Jesus' ministry. His ministry would change not only his immediate region, but also the world—even 2000 years later. In fact, billions of lives have been and are being changed by the ministry of Jesus.

At the beginning of Jesus' ministry, we find a fourfold foundation that serves as a good template for us. As we start or restart new things this year, let's learn from Jesus how to lay the proper foundation before doing anything.

Let's learn how we may start strong.

What are these four things?

First, we see that Jesus starts his ministry **affirmed.**

Secondly, we see that Jesus starts his ministry **dependent**.

Thirdly, we see that Jesus starts his ministry **proclaiming** the gospel's good news.

And finally, we see that Jesus starts his ministry **connecting people** to purpose.

Let's look at each of these four.

AFFIRMED

Jesus starts his ministry affirmed. In verses 9 through 11, we have the recorded account of Jesus' baptism. Earlier in the chapter, we can see John the Baptist beginning his ministry in the desert, calling people to repent. As men and women repented of their sins, they were baptized into this new life John called them to live; a life of holiness and proximity to God, a life that turns its back to sin and its face towards God.

Now comes Jesus. John introduces Jesus as the one who is more powerful than he, the one for whom he is not even worthy to tie or untie the sandals on his feet. So, how does Jesus begin his ministry? By meeting John out in the wilderness. Jesus goes to the river Jordan where John baptizes people and is baptized by John.

Baptism is a symbolic act, and we learn a few things as Jesus is baptized by John. First, there's a passing of the baton. John's ministry of power arrived after 400 years of prophetic silence. Then Jesus comes unto the scene and is affirmed by John. Jesus fulfills the hope present in the prophets of Israel: he is the true Messiah of whom John had spoken. This is the passing of the baton. John essentially says: "I have led people to this point. I have prepared the way. Now you are going to take them, Jesus, to the next level." When John baptized Jesus, there was prophetic fulfillment that he is the Messiah who was to come.

Moreover, Jesus not only receives affirmation from John, but something extraordinary happens at the moment of baptism: *Jesus receives confirmation from the mouth of God!* As Jesus comes out of the water, piercing the surface, the heavens open and the Spirit of God descends upon Jesus like a dove. Then a voice speaks: "You are my beloved child, of whom I am well, fully, totally pleased." The creator, God of the universe, confirmed not only that Jesus was the Messiah promised from God, but also that Jesus was God himself, the Son of God.

Jesus begins his ministry fully aware of who he is. Jesus starts his ministry from a place of affirmation, heard directly from the Father.

This is very significant for us. Many of us do not start our plans with the assurance that we are affirmed or from a place of affirmation. Instead, we start our projects *in order* to receive affirmation.

Do you see what I'm saying? **We want others to see our good deeds, our success, our development, and come to us and say, "Hey, you matter. You made it. You are somebody in this life and in this world."**

If we're honest, our need for affirmation is usually the motivator driving us to start things. Not because we *are* affirmed, but because *we want to* be affirmed. It's what Rocky Balboa used to say to his wife. Remember the Rocky movies? He said to his wife Adrian, *"Hey, listen, I want to go the distance with the champ because only then will I know that I'm not a bum."* Similarly, I remember a comment made by a New York Times writer considering his writing career. He said: *"When I made the quality of my work the measure of my worth, I set myself up for major disappointment."*

Often, we take the quality of what we do, the quality of our work, and translate that into the measure of our worth. We do all this to gain affirmation, rather than working from a foundation of affirmation.

The need for approval begins early in life. We seek the assurance of our parents: "You matter. You are good. You are loved." This understanding is important in our growth, a genuine need in life. One of the great benefits of becoming a Christian is that we are now in Christ. That's what the Bible says: You are in Christ, and all that is Christ's is now yours! Consider what the apostle Paul says in Galatians 2:11. "No longer do I live, but Christ lives in me." As Christians, the affirmation that Jesus receives from the Father becomes yours also.

God the Father looks down at Jesus and says, "There's no flaw in you. You are beautiful. You are worth it. You are loved." When you put your faith in Jesus that affirmation becomes yours. What great news! This is the gospel!

By contrast, when we think about affirmation, many people in our culture say, "Oh, all you need is to affirm yourself." But in truth, nobody can meet their need for affirmation from within themselves. We need affirmation from the outside.

So, let me ask you: What if you had the affirmation of the most important Being in the universe? What if the most important Being in the universe affirmed you, saying, "You matter, and you are worthy." Then, what if you could believe this *before* starting on your goals and plans?

The power of this truth would allow you to start from a place of affirmation. You would start strong.

What if the most important Being in the universe affirmed you, saying, **"You matter, and you are worthy."**

The first thing we learn from this passage in Mark's gospel is that Jesus starts affirmed. Do you want to start something?

Begin affirmed. Begin from that place. Start from that standpoint. You don't have to prove anything to anyone because you are already loved by the creator God of the universe. The most important opinion is already yours.

DEPENDENT

Jesus starts his ministry dependent. The next thing we read in Mark 1:12-13 is that Jesus is led by the Spirit of God into the wilderness. First, as we have seen, Jesus is baptized, coming out of the water affirmed by God. The Spirit of God comes upon him in that very moment. Then the same Spirit takes Jesus out into the wilderness, where he stays for forty days and forty nights. Jesus fasts, prays, and experiences temptation by the Devil during these days.

It is very significant what the Scripture says here: *Jesus stays in the wilderness for forty days and forty nights.* Why does this matter? Because in the Bible, the number forty is deeply meaningful. It is a number of preparation. Forty represents a time of incubation before God does something big.

For instance, when God called Moses to deliver the people from Egypt, Moses had been in the wilderness for forty years. When God leads the people out of Egypt into the Promised Land, they spend forty years in the desert. After Jesus rises from the dead, he spends forty days on earth before ascending into heaven. Moreover, forty is the number of weeks for a human pregnancy, a full gestation period.

Here is why this matters: When God takes you to a season of wilderness and puts you under this timeframe of forty, God is incubating you in the womb of the Holy Spirit.

When God incubates us in the womb of the Holy Spirit, the nutrients we need for growth are found in Jesus' way of life in the wilderness: Prayer. Prayer cultivates all the nutrients that help us grow, develop, and flourish in the wilderness while we are prepared by God for something to come. Jesus starts his ministry with prayer.

Now, many of you may have asked this question: "But isn't Jesus God? And we pray to God. So why does Jesus have to pray if he is God?" The Bible teaches us that Jesus is 100% God and is also 100% human. Jesus shares all that God the Father is, *and* our own humanity. If we follow Jesus' life through the Gospel of Mark, we will see that his path was very difficult. Jesus' life was not only marked by the work of God penetrating and transforming lives, but was also a journey marked by pain, suffering, and even betrayal. Jesus' life was marked by frustration and abandonment by the ones in whom he had invested the most. Jesus knew that life would be no easy task and, in the end, even led him to the cross. He knew, as one who was also 100% human, that he needed to depend on God the Father. He needed to depend on prayer.

Jesus never underestimated the power of the Devil. Jesus never underestimated the power of the world. Jesus never underestimated the power of the flesh. So, what makes you and I think we can underestimate these things? What makes you and I believe we can succeed in anything if we don't depend on prayer? Maybe you have the skills to take something from Point A to Point B, but do you have the emotional and spiritual strength to get yourself through when times are rough and difficult?

Do you know why so many of us quit when we're carrying out our goals? Because we are not bathed in prayer. We have not allowed God to prepare us in the womb of the Spirit through prayer. Do we want to make decisions? Do we want to set goals? Yes, we want to move forward in our own strength without dependence on God. But then we grow weary and weak. When the inevitable trials come and difficulties arise, start by becoming dependent on God and not on yourself.
Start being dependent on prayer, and you will start strong.

Start being **dependent on prayer,**

and you will start **strong.**

PROCLAIMING

Jesus starts his ministry by proclaiming the gospel. Jesus not only begins affirmed, not only starts dependent, but Jesus starts by proclaiming the gospel.

The next thing we read in Mark 1:14-15 is that Jesus came into Galilee proclaiming the gospel of God, announcing that the time is fulfilled and the kingdom of God is at hand. He calls people to repent and believe the gospel.

Notice that the word *gospel* here appears two times. First, it is the message that comes out of Jesus' mouth. Second, it is the main word coming from Jesus as he launches his earthly ministry.

What is the gospel? It is good news. The word is a translation of the Greek term *euangelion*. If you are of Latin origin like myself, then you know this word is where we get the word *evangelho* (Portuguese) and the word *evangelio* (Spanish). It's the gospel. It's good news.

This word is packed with meaning in the Bible. This is not ordinary good news, like, "Hey, I have good news. I got a raise!" Or "Good news! I went out on a date last night." No, this is not like that. Those things may be good news to you, and they may change your life, but frankly, they have no effect on *my* life. On the other hand, every time the word *euangelion* (gospel) was used, it meant a life-changing moment that you did not participate in, but which will affect your life regardless.

In ancient times, people received an *euangelion* (gospel) of Caesar Augustus when he became emperor. This meant: "Hey listen, you didn't put him in power, but he has become your emperor, and that will change your life." Or you had the *euangelion* of Julius Caesar when he went to battle and won. Heralds would stand in public places and shout, "Here is the *euangelion*. Here is the gospel of Julius Caesar. You did not go out and fight. You did not do anything, and yet he has won on your behalf, and it will affect your life positively going forth. He has eliminated your enemies on your behalf."

Similarly, every time Jesus uses the word *eu-angelion* (good news, gospel), he is saying, "I have come to alter history, and I have come to alter your life. What I have come to do, you cannot do for yourself." The Bible's use of the word *gospel* means that God has saved us; we did not do it ourselves. Salvation is of the Lord. The Lord is the one who saves!

Do you know why this is such an important message for us today, especially as we begin a new endeavor? Because we tend to think of victory as coming through our own power and strength rather than resting in who God is and what God has promised to be and do for us. In Christ, God saves us. This is the God who has vowed to take care of us, the God who has promised to always go before us.

When we believe this gospel message, we are compelled to proclaim this gospel to others. More importantly, every morning that we wake up, we ought to proclaim this gospel to ourselves. We ought to say: "Hey, I'm not the one who's going to save today. The Lord is the one who's going to save. I'm not the one who's going to provide today. The Lord is the one to provide. I'm not the one who's going to deliver today. The Lord is the one who will deliver."

If you don't preach that to your heart, you will go out the door and the culture will preach another gospel to you. When the culture preaches to you, it puts you at the center and sets you up for significant disappointment. You won't have what you truly need, which only God can give.

Remember, the victory is the Lord's. What happens when you preach the gospel to yourself every day? First, you learn that salvation is by grace. You begin to fill with a sense of humility. After all, you were not saved because you earned it or worked for it. You were saved because God chose in Jesus Christ to save you. It was given to you. It was by grace alone. Moreover, anyone who knows we are saved by grace, not by our works and merits, is someone who can never look down on anyone else. We have received salvation from God due to the grace of Jesus because we are incapable of earning it. This reality is the birthplace of humility. At the same time, this understanding inspires boldness because you are now living out of gratitude for what God has done for you. If God is for you, who can be against you?!

You are loved by God. You are loved by the most important Being in the universe. This truth fills us with courage. It fills us with boldness and the power we need to start anything. Do you see why the gospel is essential, even when we are starting something new? The gospel gives us the humility and the courage we need. So, learn to preach and proclaim the gospel to yourself, and you will start strong.

PURPOSE

Jesus starts his ministry by connecting people to purpose. Remember what we've seen so far: Jesus starts affirmed. Jesus starts dependent. Jesus starts proclaiming the gospel. Now, after preaching the gospel, Jesus passes through the towns along the sea of Galilee. **The text of Mark 1:16-18 says:**

"Passing alongside the Sea of Galilee, he saw Simon and Andrew the brother of Simon casting a net into the sea, for they were fishermen. And Jesus said to them, "Follow me, and I will make you become fishers of men.' And immediately they left their nets and followed him".

Let me ask you a question. Why are you here? I don't mean whatever place you have chosen to read this. What I mean to ask you is: Why are you here in this world? Do you know why God has placed you in this world?

Imagine Jesus walking by the Sea of Galilee when he runs into these fishermen. If somebody asked Peter, Andrew, and the others, "Hey, why are you here in this world?" they would have answered, "I'm here to make a living, I'm here to catch fish. I am here to feed people. That's my purpose in this world. That's what my dad did, that's what my grandparents did. That's why I'm here, too."

It would've been a pretty good answer. Whatever you do in this life, if you're helping people, then it is a good thing—especially if you're feeding people. Especially if you're helping feed your family and your village. These are good things.

Jesus knew this—but Jesus wanted something more for them.

Sometimes, we are content with the limited purpose in which we find ourselves. Maybe you also have a good answer like Peter and Andrew had. But let me tell you something: God wants something bigger for you. Do you believe God wants something bigger for you? God wants something bigger for you because God always wants what is best for you.

Jesus wants what is best for this group. He calls these fishermen—who would probably end their lives behind nets in a boat in this small town—and says, "Come here! What you are doing is good. But I have a bigger purpose for you. Beyond feeding people with material food, I want you to feed people with spiritual food. Beyond connecting the needs of the hungry to resources, I want you to help connect people to the heart of God."

There is no greater purpose in this world than connecting people to the heart of God, connecting people to the good news of Jesus Christ. There is no greater purpose than this call.

I myself heard this call many years ago. I was going to college, studying in an engineering program, and I had a rock band. My purpose in this world was to entertain people, have a good time with my band, design structures that wouldn't fall, and provide safe shelter for people—or so I thought. Then a group of friends said to me: "Hey, listen, there is a school in the inner city with disciplinary problems. We have this idea of starting a program on Saturdays to teach these kids the Bible. We'll teach them songs and take them out of the streets for the weekend so they don't get in trouble. Would you want to do that with us?"

I said yes.

There is no greater purpose in this world than **connecting people to the heart of God**, connecting people to the **good news of Jesus Christ.**

This group of three or four friends and I walked into the *favela*, the slum. Drug dealers thought I was buying drugs. But we started that project. Within six months, it had grown to 350 kids.

Then parents started to come, saying "My kids are singing these songs at home. They're telling us these stories. We want to hear them, too. Can we start something for adults?" We started a class for adults and a class for kids. We stayed all afternoon teaching the Bible.
Before we knew it, we were a church.

START
STRONG

As this new church community grew, I realized that I did not want to be an engineer or spend my life entertaining people from a stage. These fields of work are good; careers of all types are valuable and important. But in my case, joy fills my heart when I see people come to faith, when I see their lives transformed by the gospel. It became clear that this was my purpose.

You can find that joy too. Not everyone should become a pastor like me. By no means!

Whatever vocation God has shown you, whatever craft he has given you, whatever industry God has placed you in, may you see it as an opportunity to connect people to God.

Whether you enter into a marriage, begin to parent children, start a new job, or begin a new project, keep in your mind the desire to connect people to God. Say to yourself, "I want to connect my spouse to God every day. I want to connect my kids to God every day. I want to connect my colleagues, and the people impacted by my business to God every day. *I* want to be connected to God every day, through all of this."

This year, **let us follow Jesus.** Let us begin affirmed, dependent, preaching the gospel, and connecting to purpose. **Let us start strong.**

QUESTIONS
FOR REFLECTION

These questions are provided for you to personally engage with this topic, or you may want to meet as a small group – your girlfriends, your college mates, your family members – to discuss how these elements can assist each of you in starting strong. Whether it is a new school year, restarting a marriage or starting a new business these questions will encourage you in building a good framework for living ...and starting strong!

How much importance have you given to strong foundations before starting things in life? If you have, what have been important foundations for you?

AFFIRMED

In the book Felipe mentions a NY Times writer who saw "the quality of his work as the measure of his worth." Can you identify with this?

Do you find yourself doing things in life to attain the affirmation of others or because you are secure of your calling in life?

How can being affirmed by God be a game changer for you in life?

DEPENDENT

Do you tend to be a self sufficient person or do you seek the help of others to do things in life?

What would it look like if we would depend less on our strength and power and depend more on God's strength and power?

Do you believe prayer works? How so?

What does Jesus' prayer life teach us about the power of prayer?

PROCLAIMING

Felipe talks about the importance of the word "gospel" in the Bible. If you were to fully embrace the meaning of that word, what would be the implications to you – in your family life, your personal relationships, at work?

Felipe encourages us to preach the gospel to ourselves and others daily. Why is that important if we are to start things strong?

PURPOSE

Do you know your purpose in life? Take a few moments to reflect on this question and then write down your answers here or in a journal that you can reference from time to time.

Do you believe there's a greater purpose in life than to connect people to God? Why or why not?

How could you align what you are already doing with the purpose of connecting people to God?